OFFICIAL MONEY GUIDE
FOR TEENAGERS

CONTENTS

A Little Planning With A Big Payoff

You may not know it, but you already know how to budget. The skills you need to budget your money are the same ones you use to budget your time.

Take a typical day. After school, there's probably homework to do after band practice. You and your friends are planning to meet up. You also want to upload some pictures from the concert you went to this weekend. And, oh yes, you almost forgot—you promised to take care of your younger brother for an hour.

To get everything done, you'll need to budget your time. If you spend too long doing one thing, you'll have less time for something else. And just try telling your mom you don't have time to babysit!

Budgeting your money is a lot like budgeting your time. If you know how much money you have and you work out how you'll spend (and save) it, you've got the basics of a budget. It's not that complicated. But making a budget does take some thought. And once you have a budget worked out, the trick is to stick with it.

You'll be surprised how much a budget can help you get control of your money. When you have a handle on your money, you're much more likely to be able to do the things you want, and not have to worry where you'll get the cash.

A BALANCING ACT

Another way to think about budgeting is to picture yourself as a tight-rope walker using a long pole to keep your

THE INS AND OUTS OF A BUDGET

To work out a budget, you really need to know two things:

1. How much money you have coming in. That's your **INCOME**.

2. How much money you have going out. Those are your **EXPENSES**.

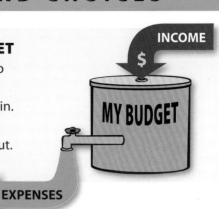

balance. Imagine that one end of the pole is income, or money you have coming in. At the other end of the pole are your expenses, or the things you spend money on. The trick is to keep your income and expenses in balance. That's what people mean when they talk about "balancing the budget."

But if one end suddenly gets heavier—let's say you have many more expenses than money to pay for them—whoops! You'll have to work hard to keep your footing. If things get really out of balance, you could topple over. Hopefully, there's a safety net—some extra money you've saved to cushion the fall.

BUDGETS GALORE

You'd be surprised how many different budgets there are. Your family probably has a budget. So does your school, your local library, and the county or city you live in. Companies have budgets, and so do the states and the federal government.

When you hear that a person or organization is in "good fiscal shape" (fiscal means "relating to money"), chances are they are spending within their budget. But if you hear that they're having "financial difficulties"

An Awkward Money Moment

BUDGET BLUNDER

Imagine you just offered to buy your friends pizza after soccer practice. You check and see that you don't have enough money in your wallet, because on Saturday you went to the movies and bought a new shirt at the mall. No problem. You figure you'll just use your pre-paid debit card. But when you try to pay, you're over your account limit. **Oh-no.** Now what?

Keep track of how you spend your money, and check your balance before you offer to be the life of the party. Avoid those awkward money moments. Check your balance often and make a habit of writing down what you spend.

or are facing default—meaning they've run out of money to cover their expenses—it means they've overspent.

While your budget may seem like small potatoes compared to these bigger budgets, guess what? The rules for making a budget—whatever the size—are exactly the same. And so are the results if you don't stick with it.

You might want to ask your parents or older family members about the ways that they budget. That could give your efforts a boost by sharing their experience with their own budget ups and downs.

INCOMING!

You might have money coming in from several different sources. For example, you might get an allowance, earn money from an after-school or weekend job, or get a gift for your birthday or other special event. The trick here is that you can count on some of this income—such as your allowance—being available on a regular basis. But getting money as a gift is less certain. It may happen,

BUDGETING GETS A BAD NAME

Budget is a word that always seems to sound negative. When you hear the word budget, you think, uh-oh, "less money for things I want," or "cutting back on spending," or "we can't afford that right now." But the truth is, budgeting isn't all that bad, and certainly not all that hard. Budgeting does mean waiting to get what you want or what you need—but not forever—just for awhile. Once you do it, you'll be surprised how little time it takes, and how big the payoff is.

but it might not. And it definitely won't happen every week or month.

So in planning your budget, you need to consider the income you can reasonably depend on, not what you hope for.

SPEND SOME, SAVE SOME

Figuring out how to spend your money in a smart way can be challenging. In fact, you might think of budgeting as a kind of game: Can you make your income cover your expenses, and still have a bit left over to save?

The savings will come in handy if you want to buy something later on, especially something expensive.

You can begin by creating two lists. One list, which we'll call **NEEDS** are those things that you simply can't do without. The second list—let's call it **WANTS**—are things you would like to have but aren't absolutely necessary.

WHAT YOU NEED

So what do you absolutely need? Well, food and clothing, for sure, and a place to live. You also need heat and electricity. While your parents may pay for a lot of these expenses, you might be responsible for some of them. For example, you might pay for your lunch on school days or use your money to buy some of the clothes you wear, such as a good coat or a sports uniform.

Some needs are a bit less certain. Do you need a phone and computer and the service plan that makes them work? You might if you use these things in school or for a job. You can probably think of a lot of other needs like these.

Now here's where the challenge comes in. While the cost of some things, like rent, are fixed—it's the same amount every month—many other costs are variable. They change based on how much you consume, such as electricity or the food you eat. You usually can choose between buying the more expensive or less expensive version of something, like a new phone, for example. Or you might buy what's on sale, or wait until something goes on sale to buy it. The more wisely you spend on the things you need, the more you'll have to spend on other things or even to save for something you need later.

WHAT YOU WANT

While you have to budget for things you need, it's also okay to budget for things that you want. These nice-to-haves may include tickets to a concert, a new app or music, lunch with friends, or buying a gift for your friend's birthday. All these expenses are variable. You can choose how much to spend and when to spend it.

There's nothing wrong with spending a part of your budget on things you'd like to have, or that are important to you. Life would be pretty dull if you didn't. The trick is to prioritize your expenses. That means deciding which things you'd like to have the most. So, if a nice present for your friend is the most important, and you have the money available in your budget, then that's where you spend it. But you want to be careful that you don't spend too much on things you want, and not have enough to pay for things you need.

MAKING CHOICES

Suppose you need a new pair of sneakers. You might have your eye on a certain pair, which might also be the most expensive. Is there a cheaper pair that you still like enough to buy? Is the store having a sale next week? If you time it right, you may be able to get the sneakers at a discount and save the difference to use later on.

Suppose you have **$200** to spend. You'd like to buy a new pair of sneakers (for **$130**, **$100**, or **$80**), a ticket to a local concert (for either **$60** or **$35**), have lunch with your friends (**$20**), and buy a present for your sister's birthday (**$35** or **$25**). Can you get everything you want for the **$200**, or will you have to give up something? That's what budgeting is all about!

SNEAKERS	+	CONCERT TICKET	+	LUNCH	+	BIRTHDAY GIFT	=	TOTAL	
$80		$35		$20		$25		$160	**$200 OR LESS**
$80		$35		$20		$35		$170	
$80		$60		$20		$25		$185	
$80		$60		$20		$35		$195	
$100		$35		$20		$25		$180	
$100		$35		$20		$35		$190	
$100		$60		$20		$25		$205	**MORE THAN $200**
$100		$60		$20		$35		$215	
$130		$35		$20		$25		$210	
$130		$35		$20		$35		$220	
$130		$60		$20		$25		$235	
$130		$60		$20		$35		$245	

BUDGETING CHOICES

You have a lot of choices about what you do with the money you have. Certainly you can spend it on needs and wants. But budgeting is more than just a spending plan. It's really a way of *allocating*, or assigning, your money to the different things you want to do and that are important to you.

Or, thinking long term, you may want to use a portion of your money to invest in the stock market or real estate, which can grow over time to provide some of the funding you'll need to pay for your education or buy a home.

You may also want to put aside some money that you can use for charity—for example, buying some cupcakes at a fundraising bake sale or making a donation to an organization that helps those in need.

You may also want to earmark some of your money for saving, which you can use to meet a short term goal, such as going on a school trip, or to pay for an unexpected expense—for example, you need to buy a phone card.

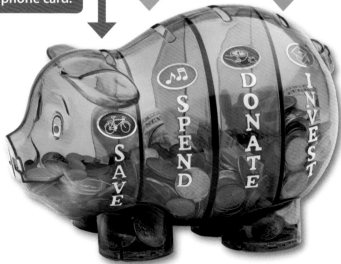

MONEY SAVVY PIG®

SAVE WHAT YOU CAN, WHEN YOU CAN

If what you spend matches what you have coming in, you have a balanced budget. Well, sort of. The problem is that you have no fallback if your expenses suddenly get higher, but

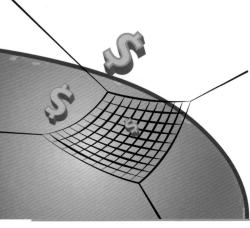

your income remains the same. Or, your expenses might remain steady, but you lose some income—let's say your allowance is cut for a week, or you don't work as many hours as you usually do and earn less as a result.

If you face this situation, which is sometimes called a budget shortfall, you can find yourself in a jam. But if you had saved part of your income and put it aside for emergencies, you would have a cushion or safety net to fall back on. Even better, if you build up the savings over time and you don't need the money for an emergency, you can use it to buy something that you really want that may cost more than your budget can other-wise handle.

STICKING WITH IT

Creating a budget is part of the story. Sticking with it is another matter. The fact is, budgets only work if you stick with them. That's because you need to keep track of both the inflow and the outflow—what's coming in and what's going out. And that can change every week or every month. Once you set up the budget categories for income and expenses, it's a matter of keeping an eye on the actual numbers.

You might want to use an app or other program to help with your budgeting. Here's one you may want to check out: **mint.com**

SAMPLE BUDGET

Let's see how a sample budget might work. The chart below lists the sources of income, or where the money is coming from, and the expenses, or where the money is being spent. Your income and expenses are probably different, and you may want to prepare your own budget using this model.

CURRENT MONTHLY BUDGET		
INCOME	**Job Earnings**	**$200**
	Allowance	**$60**
Total Monthly Earning		**$260**
EXPENSES/ ALLOCATION	**Food:** **School lunch** **Snacks** **Meals out**	**$50** **$25** **$45**
	Clothing	**$50**
	Bus or subway pass	**$12**
	Phone/Internet	**$30**
	Entertainment (music, movies, downloads)	**$25**
	Savings	**$13**
	Charity	**$10**
Total Monthly Spending		**$260**

Saving Smarts, Investing Intelligence

BENJAMIN FRANKLIN

If you've ever put loose change in a piggy bank, or stuck a few dollars in a hiding place, you know what it means to save. Instead of spending that money right away, you put it away to use another day. How much you save, and where you save it, will determine how much money you'll have when you need it.

You may wonder why saving is such a big deal.

Well, for starters, it's a great feeling to meet a short-term goal, like buying a new bike or throwing a party for a friend with money YOU saved.

Saving teaches you to live on less than you earn so you can have a nest egg to take care of your wants or needs in the future.

Savings are also a safety net, in case some unexpected expenses come

So how much should you save? That depends on your budget. First you need to see how much money you have left after you pay for the things you need. Then you'll need to decide how much money you'll spend on things you want. But you should always budget at least a small amount for saving, even if it means waiting a bit to get something you really want.

So how much should you save? Set a goal that makes sense for you. Saving 5% of the money that you get on a regular basis is a great place to start. The more you can save the better, especially if you are saving for a specific goal, or if you have money left over in your budget.

A PENNY SAVED IS A PENNY EARNED.

up—like needing to replace a phone or school book that you lost. People sometimes call this money an emergency fund or rainy day fund. It's money you can put your hands on quickly when you need it.

SAFE PLACES TO SAVE

Saving money in your sock drawer or under your mattress is better than not saving at all. But it's always risky to leave money around, even if your hiding place seems very secure.

If your money is easy to get to, there's always the temptation to spend it. Even if you plan to pay it back, there's a good chance you'll never get around to replacing what you took from your savings.

The real issue, though, is that keeping your money in your room doesn't do much for you. The money just sits there. But if you deposit that money in a bank or credit union, it can actually earn you more money. That's because a **savings account** pays you **interest** on your money. The higher the interest the account pays, and the longer you keep saving, the more money you'll earn.

Now you know what Benjamin Franklin meant when he said: "A penny saved is a penny earned."

QUIZ: WHERE IS THE BEST PLACE TO SAVE YOUR MONEY?

WITHOUT A BANK ACCOUNT

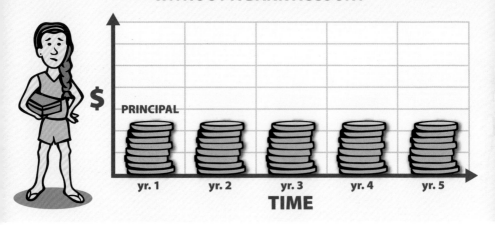

PRINCIPAL

yr. 1   yr. 2   yr. 3   yr. 4   yr. 5

TIME

INTERESTED YET?

Instead of working for your money, how about having your money work for you? That's what earning interest is all about. The bank or credit union pays you interest on your **principal**, which is the amount you deposit in your account.

If the bank pays you **simple interest**, you earn money only on your principal. For example, if you have $100 in your account and it pays simple interest of 2% a year, you would earn $2, and end up with $102.

But if the bank pays you **compound interest**, the interest you earn is usually calculated daily and added to your principal monthly or quarterly, creating a new, larger principal. And since interest is paid on a bigger

An Awkward Money Moment

SAVE OR SPEND?

You've been really proud of yourself for putting away $10 every week to save up for your new soccer uniform. You've got three more weeks to reach your goal before the season starts. But your best friend wants you to go to the amusement park this Saturday, and paying for a day of rides, food, and souvenirs will completely wipe out the money you've saved up. Do you say no to your friend, or decide to wear your old uniform another year?

Sometimes, an awkward money moment can happen when you're trying to be financially responsible. Chances are, if you explain to your friend that you're saving up for something important, she'll understand. And you'll feel great when you reach your savings goal. And your savings stash gave you the option of going in the first place!

A BANK ACCOUNT WITH COMPOUND INTEREST (%)

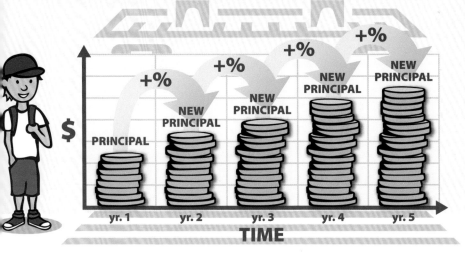

principal each time, you earn more each time too.

Thanks to compounding, the earlier you start saving, and the higher the interest rate you earn, the more money you'll end up with. If you wait to start saving—even if you put in more money later on—it's very hard to ever catch up.

SAVINGS CHOICES

Just as you have choices in making your budget, you also have choices when it comes to saving. Banks and credit unions offer different types of accounts, and each pays a different rate of interest.

There are trade-offs. Accounts that give you greater flexibility generally pay lower interest rates. Accounts that pay higher interest often have some restrictions. You'll also need to consider how much you're going to deposit, and how long you plan to keep the money in the account.

Regular Savings Accounts.
Regular savings accounts generally pay a lower rate of interest than you might earn on other accounts. But you can deposit or withdraw money whenever you want. This easy access is called **liquidity** and it means you can get cash quickly and without penalty.

If you're saving for a short term goal—say you're planning to go on your school's spring trip a few months from now—a regular savings account may be your best bet. It's also ideal if you're putting money aside for emergencies.

One thing to check out first: You may need a certain amount to open the account and to keep it open in order to qualify to earn interest and avoid fees. A good tip is to look for special student accounts.

13

Certificates of Deposit. A certificate of deposit, or CD, generally pays a higher rate of interest than a savings account, but it's not as liquid. That's because each CD has a term— for example, three, six, or nine months—and you need to keep your money in the CD for the entire term. If you take your money out early, you'll forfeit, or lose, some or all of the interest you've earned.

Also, you might need several hundred dollars to open a CD. But if you know you won't need the money for a while, and would like to earn a higher interest rate, a bank CD might be the way to go.

Money Market Account. A money market account pays a higher rate of interest than a regular savings account. But you'll probably need at least an average daily balance of $1,000 or more to qualify for the interest and avoid fees. So you might consider this kind of savings account if you get a large amount of money—maybe as a birthday or graduation gift.

While money market accounts are liquid, they aren't as flexible as regular savings accounts. There may be a limit on the number of transactions you can make each month. And if you don't keep a certain amount of money, or **balance**, in the account, the bank may charge you a fee or not pay any interest.

GOTCHA COVERED!

One other thing to know about saving accounts—they're safe. That's because the federal government insures your account up to $250,000. So even if something happens to your bank or credit union, the federal government will cover your savings up to that amount.

KEEPING UP WITH THE COST OF THINGS

When it comes to money, older people are probably always telling you how cheap things used to be, and how expensive they are now. They remember when it cost just a dime to take a bus, or a couple of dollars to go to the movies. You're sure to hear that a dollar is not worth what it used to be.

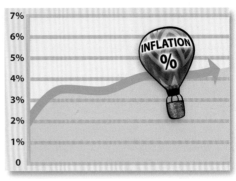

Actually, they're right. This increase in the cost of things over time is called **inflation**. Sometimes inflation is high, and prices can increase 6% or more each year. At other times, inflation can be as low as 1%, or even less. Because of inflation, the dollars you have today won't buy you as much tomorrow. So you'll need even more money to buy the same things.

The way to beat inflation is to make sure that your money is earning more than the rate of inflation. For example, if inflation is 2%, you'll want your savings to be earning at least 3%. However, that's almost never the case. Savings accounts almost always pay less than inflation, whatever the current rate of inflation. So what can you do? Save until you can invest!

THE RULE OF 72

One way to compare savings to investing is to use the Rule of 72. According to this rule, you can figure out how long it will take to double your money. You divide 72 by your earnings rate. For example, if your savings account is earning 3% interest, you would divide 72 by 3 which equals 24. So it would take 24 years to double your money. But if you were earning a 6% return on your investments, you would double your money in just 12 years (72 ÷ 6 = 12).

Investing does involve **risk**, however. You could lose some or all of the money you've invested. That's because investments aren't insured the way bank or credit union accounts are.

As a rule, the greater the risk you take with an investment, the more potential there is for a higher return. But higher risk means there's also a greater chance you could lose your money. Remember that balancing act from making a budget? When you invest, you're looking for a balance between risk and return.

$$\frac{72}{\% \text{ interest rate}} = \text{Years to double your money}$$

$$\frac{72}{6\%} = 12 \text{ Years}$$

15

INVESTING IN YOUR FUTURE

To keep ahead of inflation, many people **invest** some of their money instead of just saving it. Investing is another way your money can work for you. While saving is ideal for meeting short-term goals, investing is better for long-term goals, like paying for college or buying a home. That's because when you invest your money, it needs time to grow.

When you invest, you are looking for a good **return**. The return is the amount of money you make on an investment. As a rule, you get a better return on investments than on savings accounts.

THE CHOICE IS YOURS

When you pick a savings account, you look for one that pays a high interest rate. When it comes to investments, it's even more important that you do your research. For each investment you are considering, find out as much as you can. Most of the information is available online at the websites of the companies offering the investments.

You want to be as sure as you can that the investment is solid and has a good chance of providing a strong return.

There are many kinds of investments you can choose from, but by far the most common are stocks, bonds, mutual funds, and real estate. Each of these has a different level of risk and different potential for return.

Stocks. You can invest in the stock market by buying shares of stock in a public company. When you hold the shares, you actually own a piece of the company. You can make money on a stock if you sell it for a higher price than you paid for it. A company may also pay its shareholders dividends.

How Do You Choose a Stock to Buy?

- Pick a company you like and respect or admire.

- Learn more about how this company earns money and if it is profitable.

- See if you can find out the company's plans to grow bigger and better.

- Find out if the company has any competitors, and if they are better than the competition.

- Make a plan to keep track of the company's profits and stock price.

Bonds. Federal and state governments sell bonds when they need to raise cash for a public project, like building schools, roads, or libraries. Private companies also issue bonds to raise **capital**, or money, for development and growth.

Each bond pays interest at a specific rate until it **matures**, or comes due. You then get back your principal, which is the money you used to buy the bond, plus the interest you've earned.

Bonds are generally less risky than stocks, because their prices are less **volatile**, meaning they don't change as quickly or as often. However, historically, bonds have also paid a lower rate of return than stocks.

Mutual Funds. Mutual funds own stocks or bonds, or a combination of the two, and can be a great place to start as an investor. When you buy shares in a mutual fund, you own a small percentage of the fund. You can make money investing in a fund by buying shares at one price and then selling them at a higher price. The fund may also earn dividends or interest that is passed on to you.

Funds are generally less risky than stocks because the risk is spread across a number of different investments that fund owns. Also, each fund has a professional manager who buys and sells the fund's investments, so you know there is someone looking after the fund all the time.

As with all investments, however, mutual funds can lose value. So be sure to read the fund prospectus, which tells you all about the fund, including what investments it makes and the fees the fund charges while you own its shares.

INVESTMENT CLUBS

Consider starting a "pretend-money" investment club. Each member researches a company that the club would like to invest in. Decide how much of your pretend money to invest in each company. At your monthly meetings, talk about how your "investments" are performing. You can also go online and read all about investment clubs that invest real money, and how they work.

Cash, Credit, Debit: Choose the Right Way to Pay

When you buy something, you have to decide how you're going to pay for it.

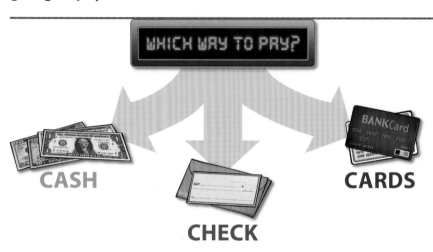

WHICH WAY TO PAY?

CASH

CHECK

CARDS

For small things, like a snack, you'll probably pay cash. But for more expensive purchases or for when you don't have money with you, a debit or credit card can be handy. There are also ways to pay that can save you money and even earn you rewards.

Each type of payment has certain advantages, but also certain risks or sometimes added costs. Being smart about how to pay is another way to use your money wisely.

CASH IN HAND

Cash is money, or **currency**. The person you pay in cash can use that money to pay someone else. This system works because people agree on the value of the currency. Dollars, quarters, dimes, nickels, and pennies all have a specific worth so people can use them to buy things with a specific price.

Cash certainly is convenient, but it does have a few drawbacks. It's easy to misplace money, and it can be stolen. You may get the wrong change and not realize it. Also, unless you always get a receipt, there's no record of what you paid, so it's harder to keep track of your expenses.

CHECK IT OUT

You open a **checking account** with a bank or credit union by depositing money into the account. You can then withdraw money, write checks, use a debit card, or have money drawn directly from your account to make purchases or to pay monthly expenses such as rent, utilities like electricity, or loan repayments. You just have to be sure you have **available funds**, or enough money in your account to cover what you spend.

A real plus of having your money in a checking account is that it is insured by the Federal Deposit Insurance Corporation (FDIC). That means that it is safe, even if something happens to the bank where you have your account. Even better, some checking accounts pay interest on your balance. And most banks offer special accounts with lower costs for students.

Since banks charge fees for checking accounts, look for one that charges the lowest amount for the services you want. So ask about their fees for:

• The number of checks you plan to write each month

Some people don't have bank accounts. Instead, they use other services to cash their checks and pay their bills, almost always paying more for these services than a bank would charge if they had an account. Another problem with this approach: They're not building relationships or credit histories with banks that might help them get a loan or offer them a credit card in the future.

• Account balances that fall below a required minimum

• Using an ATM

• Paying your bills online

Picking the right checking account is another way to make the most of your money.

COMPARING BANK FEES

NUMBER OR CODE	DATE	TRANSACTION DESCRIPTION	PAYMENT AMOUNT	✓	FEE	DEPOSIT AMOUNT	$
101	9/12	Phone bill	$ 45			$	532.29
	9/14	Babysitting check				80	612.29
102	9/15	Soccer jersey	38				574.29

WRITING CHECKS

Each check has a number, which you should record in your checkbook **register** each time you write a check. The checks you write are also reported on your monthly statement. Since checks provide a record of what you are spending, they can help you stay within your budget. If you lose a check, be sure to notify the bank to cancel it so that nobody else can cash it.

Never sign a check and leave the other information blank—especially the amount and the "Pay To" line. A signed check is like cash once it has your signature on it.

KEEPING THINGS IN CHECK

When you deposit cash into your account, it's available right away. But it's important to remember that when you deposit a check, it may take several days to be fully credited to your account. So make sure the money is really in your account before you write a new check or make a payment. Otherwise, the check may **bounce**, or the payment denied because of **insufficient funds**. When a check bounces, the bank will charge you a fee, and the company or person that deposited your check may also be charged a fee when they deposit the check in their own account.

When you send a check by mail, remember that it may take several days to reach the person or company you're paying. If your payment is late, you may owe an additional fee. The late payment may also be noted on your credit report and hurt your credit score. Timing your deposits and payments is a key to using checking wisely.

PAY TO THE ORDER OF

An Awkward Money Moment

RETURN TO SENDER

Few things are more embarrassing than having the bank return a check for "insufficient funds." The person or company who received the check and was charged a fee for depositing it is justifiably angry, and you feel terrible because you wrote the check believing it would clear.

 You can avoid this type of awkward moment by keeping track of the checks in your register and writing checks only when you know for sure the balance is high enough to cover them.

Your bank may also offer you **overdraft protection**, which is a special line of credit that's used to pay your bills if you overdraw your account. While there is often a fee when you use this service, it's probably worth it to avoid bouncing a check.

OVERDRAFT PROTECTION FOR CHECKING ACCOUNTS

While overdraft protection for a debit card is probably not a good idea—when money is gone, it is gone—it can be a handy strategy when it comes to a checking account. The fees for that type of overdraft protection are usually much smaller, and it can prevent you from bouncing a check or having insufficient funds for a monthly payment, such as rent.

DEBIT CARDS

If you use a card to purchase something in a store, the check-out clerk will probably ask you, "Debit or credit?" Or you might see these options when you swipe your card to complete a purchase. So which one do you choose?

When you use a **credit card**, the charge will be billed to your credit card account and won't be due until a specified number of days after it appears on your statement.

If you use a **debit card**, however, the amount of your purchase is deducted directly from your bank account. You may make a debit charge by using your **PIN** (personal identification number) or by signing a receipt. You can also use your debit card to make payments by phone, to buy things online, and to get money from an ATM.

If you don't have enough money in your account, a debit purchase won't go through. But if you have agreed to have overdraft protection, the bank will cover the amount you are short, though they'll charge you interest and a fee. You should think seriously about turning down the protection, though, because it will help you to limit overspending and stay within your budget.

When you sign up for a debit card, check to see if the bank charges a fee every time you use your debit card with a PIN.

If you make a lot of debit card purchases, those fees can add up very quickly. Some stores may also charge you extra transaction fees for using debit and ATM cards. You should also find out what they charge for making cash withdrawals with your card. Those costs can be very high, especially if you use machines your bank doesn't own.

Be especially careful about using a debit card to charge certain costs that are not fixed, such as gas for your car. The retailer may charge you twice— once for an estimated amount, which you eventually get back, and again for the actual cost of the gas. If the combined charges overdraw your account, you could end up owing additional fees.

Debit and ATM cards are a convenient way to pay, but their fees can be pricey. The more you pay in fees, the less you'll have to spend on other things.

It's easy to confuse a debit card with an **ATM card**, also called a bank card. That's because you can use your ATM card to make certain purchases by swiping your card and entering your PIN. But you can't use your ATM card to pay by phone or online, or in situations where you need to sign your name. One way to tell the difference is to look at the card. If you see the bank name only, it's an ATM card. But if you see the bank identity and also the VISA or MasterCard logo, then it's a debit card.

APPS CAN PAY, TOO

For people on the go, some banks offer apps you can use to view your account balance and pay your bills. With the app on your phone or tablet, you can pay whenever and wherever you are. You can also download apps that you can use like a debit card. Instead of swiping your card, you scan the app to make a purchase.

have different policies. A good place to research the differences is Bankrate.com.

THIS CARD HAS ITS LIMITS

If you like using a debit card but don't want to overspend, check out a **prepaid debit card**. You use it just like a regular debit card. But you can spend only the amount that's loaded onto the card. So you never have to worry about overdrawing your account.

The tradeoff is that prepaid debit cards may have large fees. Be sure to check how much it costs to use the card. Another good question to ask: What happens to my balance if the card is lost or stolen? Banks

ONLINE PAYMENTS

It's quick and easy to pay bills and shop online. But there are certain risks, such as someone stealing your security codes and your money.

Many checking accounts let you pay your bills online. You set up a list of **payees**—usually the companies and people you pay on a regular basis. When a bill comes due, you indicate the amount due to the payee and the date you want the bill paid. Since it may take a few days to process the transaction, be sure to leave enough time so your payments won't be late.

You can also pay by **direct debit**, which lets a payee take money directly from your account to pay your bill. Direct debit works well for regular bills, such as rent or cable service, but not so well for bills that can change from month to month, such as an electric or gas bill. There's always the chance that a large bill, especially one you don't expect, will overdraw your account.

A safer way to pay is to authorize a company to debit your account only for the amount that you specify when you initiate the payment. That way, you can make sure your balance is large enough to cover the bill. And it's a good way to keep an eye on your monthly expenses.

ELECTRONIC MONEY

As e-commerce has grown, so have the ways you can pay for things online. Besides your credit and debit cards, you might use an online payment company, such as **popmoney** or **PayPal**, to pay your bills, make purchases, or even send gifts electronically.

Since accounts with these companies are linked to your bank or credit card, you never have to share your account numbers when paying online. That's a real plus and can help protect your financial information from fraud. But there may be a fee for using these services and other limitations, such as the number of transactions you can make each month. While "electronic wallets" are convenient and secure, they may not always be your best payment choice.

COUPONS

Coupons let you buy things at a special discount. Companies offer coupons to promote their products and build your loyalty as a customer. In addition to traditional paper coupons that you can use at grocery and drug stores, most online stores offer limited-time discounts or free shipping. It's worth timing your purchases to take advantage of these offers. You may also want to check out sites and services that offer coupons for a range of stores. They can be a smart way to save some money.

GIFT CARDS

Some of the money you have might be on prepaid **gift cards**, which you may have received for your birthday or a holiday. If the gift card is issued by a credit card company, you can use it for a variety of purchases in different places. However, cards issued by a particular store or service provider— for example, a clothing store or a phone company—can be used only to buy things from that company.

Gift cards are a lot like cash. They're easy to use, but easy to lose. And if they're lost or stolen, they're often gone for good. Some also have fees and expiration dates, so be sure to check the details. And you have to keep track of your balance on the card. Otherwise, you might think you have enough left to make a purchase, and end up having to spend out of your own pocket.

REWARD YOURSELF

You already know that you can earn money on your savings. But did you know that you can also earn things when you spend? That's what you're doing when you pay with points or other rewards you've earned from loyalty programs.

You can sign up for loyalty programs with retail stores, online merchants, hotel chains, and airlines. Usually, there's no cost to join. Each time you buy something from that company, you earn points based on the amount you spend. When you accumulate enough points, you can redeem or exchange the points for a gift, free stay, free flight, or even cash.

Another kind of loyalty card is the kind given out by stores and restaurants, where they reward you for making a certain number of purchases. For example, a smoothie shop might give you your tenth smoothie for free, after you've bought nine.

If you stick with a loyalty program long enough, you may be able to purchase something that you couldn't otherwise afford. But it can take a long time to build up enough points to make it worthwhile. And you want to be careful about buying things just to get the points, instead of buying things you really need or that you can buy for less somewhere else.

27

Only Borrow What You Can Pay Back Tomorrow

Swipe a credit card. You just paid for something without taking a penny out of your pocket. What could possibly be wrong with that? Actually, quite a few things, if you don't understand how to use credit in a responsible way.

When you use a credit card, you are using someone else's money. Typically that someone else is a bank, a credit union, or other financial company that issued you the card. That's okay, as long as you can pay back all your card charges when your payment is due. If you do, your credit card becomes a very convenient way to pay for things, such as items you order online, where you can't use cash.

But if you don't pay back the full amount you owe—called your **balance**—the bank will charge you interest on the amount you don't repay. To make matters worse, you'll also owe interest on any new purchases you make. As you charge more but don't repay the full amount

you owe, that interest just keeps growing, and growing, and growing.

The bottom line is that using credit cards can end up costing you more, sometimes a lot more, than paying in cash. But if you know how to use credit cards wisely, then credit can actually work for you, not against you.

A MATTER OF INTEREST

How does credit actually work? The first thing to know is that **credit** is really **debt**. When you use credit, you are borrowing money from the bank or company that issued you the card.

Your card has a **credit limit**. You can spend up to that limit, and when you pay back an amount that you owe, that amount is available to borrow again. That's called **revolving credit**.

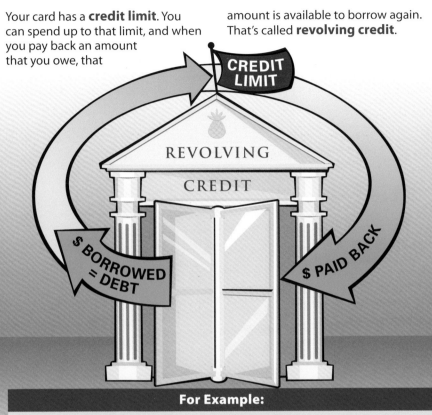

CREDIT LIMIT

REVOLVING CREDIT

$ BORROWED = DEBT

$ PAID BACK

For Example:

Suppose your credit card has a **$2,000 limit.**
You spend **$800** one month.

Your available credit is now only **$1,200** ($2,000 – $800).

But if you pay back that $800 by the time your credit card payment is due, the full limit, or $2,000, is available to spend again.

CREDIT CAN COST YOU

One of the most important things to look for in the credit agreement that you sign is the **grace period**. This is the time you have to pay your credit card bill before the issuer starts charging you interest. If you pay the full amount by the end of the grace period, you won't owe any interest. Remember, though, it's not enough to just send your payment by the due date. You need to leave enough time to be sure that the company actually receives your payment by that day. That's a smart way to use your credit card. It's also smart to shop around for a card that has a grace period, since not all cards do.

If you don't pay the full amount due, the grace period no longer applies. So you'll start paying interest as soon you make a new charge. That means every new item you charge is automatically costing you more.

However, if you make a mistake, or if you are only able to pay the minimum amount due one month, all is not lost. You can get your grace period benefit back. Pay the full amount due and the grace period ultimately will be reinstated.

Another thing you'll discover is that your credit card has an **APR**, or annual percentage rate. This is the rate that the credit card issuer will charge you on any amounts you don't repay in full when they are due. The higher the APR, the more interest you'll pay.

APRs can vary from card to card. So in choosing your credit card, be sure to find one with a low APR. Even a small difference can add up to a lot of money when it comes to paying off debt.

FEES TO AVOID

One way that credit card issuers make money is by letting you pay the **minimum amount due** each month. If you pay only the minimum amount due, or anything less than the full amount you owe, you'll have to pay a **finance charge** on the **unpaid balance**.

The finance charge is determined by the APR and the size of your unpaid balance. The higher your interest rate, and the larger your unpaid balance, the more you'll owe.

But be sure to pay at least the minimum amount by the due date. If you pay late or not at all, you'll be charged a big fee. And your APR will probably go up. That means borrowing will cost you even more.

Some cards also charge an annual fee, just to have the card. This fee can vary

CREDIT CARD PROTECTIONS

The Fair Credit Billing Act and certain government agencies help protect you against unfair credit card practices and establish your card rights. It pays to visit **www.federalreserve.gov** and read about credit protection laws when you start using a credit card. That way, you'll know what rights you have, and what to do, if you have a problem with your card issuer.

There are a few key things you can do to protect yourself. Always keep receipts of your credit charges and compare them to the amounts shown on your statement. If there is a charge you didn't make, notify the card issuer immediately. That way, the issuer can determine if someone is using your card illegally. In case of fraud, the issuer may cancel your card and send you a new one. Report the loss of your credit card immediately.

If you discover an error that you can't get resolved, or you feel you are being treated unfairly, you can file a complaint at the Consumer Financial Protection Bureau at **www.consumerfinance.gov**.

a lot from card to card, and some card issuers don't charge one at all. So it's worth it to shop around and find a card that doesn't have an annual fee. That way, you'll keep the cost of using credit as low as possible.

THE SNOWBALL EFFECT

Think of credit card interest as a snowball rolling down a steep hill. The snowball starts out fairly small. But the longer it keeps going, the bigger it becomes. Quicker than you realize, it can get out of control.

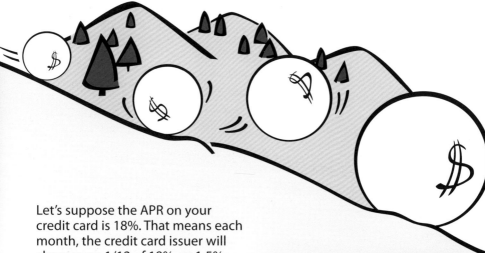

Let's suppose the APR on your credit card is 18%. That means each month, the credit card issuer will charge you 1/12 of 18%, or 1.5% of your unpaid balance. If your statement shows that you owe $550 and you pay only the minimum amount due of $25, you'll owe 1.5% of the unpaid balance of $525, which is $7.87 (.015 x $525).

While this may not seem like much, let's see what happens the following month. Let's assume that you charge another $550. The credit card issuer will apply the finance charge to the unpaid balance of $532.87 plus the new balance of $550. So your new finance charge is $16.24 (.015 x $1082.87) and you still owe all of the unpaid balance as well. Each month that you don't pay the full amount due, your finance charge will keep growing.

THIS MONTH	
Your Balance	$550
Minimum Amount Due	− $25
Unpaid Balance	$525
18% APR	X 1.5%
Finance Charges	= $7.87

NEXT MONTH	
Your Balance	$532.87
New Charges	+ $550
Unpaid Balance	= $1,082.87
18% APR	X 1.5%
Finance Charges	= $16.24

Remember the value of compounding when it comes to earning interest on your savings? When it comes to *paying* interest rather than *earning* interest, however, compounding is not your friend, but your enemy. The more interest you owe, and the longer you owe it, the more it compounds. As more of your budget goes to pay off debt, the less you have to pay for the things you need and want.

Your credit card bill will have a chart showing how much your balance will cost you if you pay only the minimum due each time. The chart assumes you don't make any new charges. It's a real eye-opener.

An Awkward Money Moment

KNOW YOUR LIMITS

Let's say you're out to dinner with friends and you try to use your credit card to pay the bill. But your card is rejected because you've exceeded your credit limit. And since you're paying for food that you've already eaten, you can't return it. Now that's embarrassing.

You can avoid this type of awkward moment by carefully checking your credit card statement each month. That way, you'll know how much credit you still have available.

LOANS ARE A KIND OF CREDIT

When you need to borrow a large amount of money to pay for a major expense, like going to college, you'll need a different kind of credit, called a loan. You apply for a loan from a bank, credit union, or other lender. Before approving a loan, the lender will ask to look at all your (or your family's) financial records, to make sure that you'll be able to repay the money you are borrowing.

Loans make it possible to pay for things you can't afford now, but that can help you get ahead or live better. For example, if you take a student loan to pay for college, your degree can help you get a better job with higher pay. Or, your family may borrow money from a bank to buy a house. Besides being a nice place to live, the house may increase in value over time, so your family can sell it at profit.

When you take a **loan**, you agree to pay back the amount you borrow, which is the **principal**, plus interest you pay on the principal. A loan typically has a **term**, such as 5, 10, or even 30 years. You make monthly payments during the term until you've paid off the principal and interest.

PRINCIPAL ➕ INTEREST
≡ AMOUNT YOU OWE

CHOOSING A CARD

Like clothes, phones, and cars, credit cards come in different styles with different prices. We already talked about looking for a card with a low APR and low (or no) annual fee. You might consider a card that has features especially useful for you.

Affinity cards. You might be tempted to get an affinity card, which lets you earn points or airline miles, or get cash back, for the charges you make to the card. Some of these cards may give a percentage of what you spend to a charity. But remember, it can take a long time to build enough of these benefits to make it worth your while. Affinity cards may also have fees and other restrictions.

Charge cards. You use a charge card the same way you use a credit card. But there's one major difference. You have to pay the entire amount you charged every month. You can't just pay a minimum or postpone paying the unpaid balance until next month. If you need the flexibility of paying only part of what you owe each month, a charge card is probably not a good choice.

Secured credit cards. You might apply for a secured credit card if you can't get a regular credit card. A secured card requires you to deposit money into a savings account that is linked to the card. The amount of the deposit, which you can't withdraw, is the same as your credit card limit. If you don't pay your bill, the bank takes the money from the savings account to pay what you owe. Secured cards often have lots of fees and may not help you get a regular card.

PARENTAL APPROVAL

If you are under 18 years old, you will almost always need your parent's or guardian's signature to get a credit card in your name. That means they agree to cover your bill if you don't pay. You can help out by checking out different card choices ahead of time to see which ones have low APRs, low fees, and a grace period.

YOUR CREDIT HAS A HISTORY

Your credit card payments and other loan payments are recorded by **credit rating agencies**. The three main agencies—Experian, Equifax, and TransUnion—create **credit reports** that show whether or not you are paying off your credit bills on time. They also record payments that you missed.

A credit report contains a huge amount of information about how you use credit—everything from which credit cards are in your name, what loans you have, how much you owe, and whether you pay on time.

The agencies use this information to calculate your FICO score, which can range from 300 to 850. The higher the number, the better the score. The average number is 720. Companies that lend you money, such as banks, credit unions, and credit card issuers, look at your FICO score to determine your **creditworthiness**. If they think you are a credit risk, and that you may not repay, they may decide to charge you a higher interest rate, or not give you credit at all.

Employers, landlords, or insurance companies may also check your FICO score to see how responsible you are when it comes to using credit. So having a good **credit history** is important for your financial well-being and also for your career.

If you have a low FICO score, there are ways to improve your credit rating. You can start by paying your credit card bills on time and working out a plan to use less credit until you are caught up. But continue to use your card to show that you can use credit responsibly.

The pioneering credit score company, FICO was founded in 1956 as Fair, Isaac and Company by engineer Bill Fair and mathematician Earl Isaac. The company changed its name to FICO more than fifty years later.

You can check your **credit report** for free each year with each of the three agencies by going to **www.annualcreditreport.com**. Credit agencies do make mistakes, so if you see something wrong, you should get in touch with the agency immediately to get the problem fixed.

FICO SCORE
820
VERY GOOD

Protecting Your Identity

If someone steals your money, you feel bad or angry, but there is a limit to how much you've lost. But if someone steals your identity, you could lose a lot more—and face a huge hassle as well.

The evil character Iago in William Shakespeare's play Othello understands this very well. He tells Othello:

> *Who steals my purse steals trash ...*
> *But he that filches (steals) ...*
> *my good name ...*
> *makes me poor indeed.*

Iago is talking about ruining someone's reputation. But his words can also apply to stealing your identity for fraudulent purposes—which can ruin your financial reputation. That can open the door to a lot of problems, some of which can be very hard to fix.

Identity theft is a threat to anyone who has a checking account or a debit or credit card, or who pays for things online. Even using an ATM or opening an email can expose you to financial fraud.

There are many ways that people can steal your identity. Fortunately, there are always things you can do to protect it. So it's important to know how these frauds work, and what you can do to avoid them.

Just think of identity theft as a battle of wits. The thief is trying to steal your identity. You're trying to prevent that from happening by protecting your personal information.

ID YOUR IDENTITY

Your identity is not just your name, your birthday, and where you live. Your identity is also a series of numbers and codes that organizations use to identify and recognize you.

For example, your **Social Security number** is part of your identity. So are the numbers of your bank account and your debit and credit card. The PIN you use to get cash from an ATM, as well as the user ID and password you use to log on to websites, are also part of your identity.

Because your information is electronically stored, a scammer needs just a little information about you to connect the dots and find out a lot more. That's where the trouble begins.

WHY STEAL YOUR IDENTITY, ANYWAY?

Why would someone want to steal your identity in the first place? There are lots of reasons. Here are just some of the things an identity thief might do:

- Make purchases using an illegally manufactured debit or credit card containing your account information

- Withdraw money from your banking or savings account

- Apply for new credit cards and loans in your name

- Wreck your credit history and credit score

The worst thing is, often you don't know your identity's been stolen until after it's gone. Meanwhile, the thief has used your information to get your money and buy things with your credit.

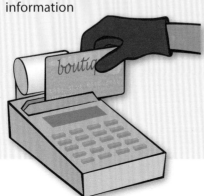

THEM vs. *YOU*

Identity thieves are very clever and have many ways to get your information. But for every trick they have up their sleeve, you can take steps to defeat them.

Pickpockets. An identify thief may steal your wallet or purse, or take personal documents from your home.

Defeat them: Take only the cards and forms of ID you absolutely need. Leave all other cards, checks, and IDs—like your Social Security number—at home, hidden in a safe place. Don't leave them lying around, even at home. And *never* attach your PIN to your debit or credit card.

Skimmers. Some identity thieves are skilled at **skimming**. They steal your credit or debit card number as your card is swiped through a processing machine.

Defeat them: Frequently check your statements or online account activity to make sure that all of the charges are ones that you made, and that the amounts are correct.

Dumpster divers: Identity thieves may sift through your mail or trash to find bills, bank and credit card statements, new checks, or credit card offers.

Defeat them: Shred all documents that show your account information that thieves could use to open a new account in your name or take money out of an existing one. Always put bills you are paying directly in a mailbox, or mail them at the post office—don't leave them for pickup in your home mailbox.

ATM Peekers. Some identity thieves peek over your shoulder when you're using an ATM to get your PIN number. They may even set up mini-cams to record you keying in your number.

Defeat them: Shield your PIN so others can't see it as you type it in. Don't assume that anyone nearby is just another person waiting to use the ATM.

An Awkward Money Moment

EMPTY POCKETS!

You're at the checkout counter about to pay for a new jacket. But you can't find your wallet anywhere—it's lost or stolen. Do you tell the clerk what happened? How embarrassing is that!

This is not a time to panic, but to act. Check if anyone has turned in your wallet to the lost and found. Think of where you last used the wallet. Could it be there? If you're sure it's been stolen, notify your bank and credit card issuer. They will invalidate the cards and issue you new ones. It's also a good idea to report the theft to the police. You may need the report number to help resolve the problems that could result.

GUARDING YOUR IDENTITY ONLINE

You can do just about anything related to money on the Internet— you can open accounts, make purchases, and pay your bills online. But the Internet also provides tons of opportunities for thieves to steal your identity.

One clever scheme, called **phishing**, tricks you into giving your username, passwords, and credit card information. Typically, these thieves will send you an email pretending to be a bank, store, or social media site. They may even create a phony website that looks like the real one. Once you enter the information they request, your identity is at risk.

But you can outsmart them by taking a few basic precautions:

39

1 Never share your contact information with anyone, especially not in an email. That includes your login, password, birthday, Social Security number and other personal information. A legitimate company will never ask for this information online, so don't provide it.

sTr0n9
P@S$wOrD

2 Don't use the same username and passwords over and over. And make them hard to decipher by mixing upper and lower case letters, adding numerals and punctuation marks, and using at least eight characters.

https://

3 Always look for a padlock or key icon to be sure you are on a secure page when you make a credit or debit card transaction. That way you'll know your card information is encrypted.

4 Make sure your computer has the most recent anti-virus software.

Internet Café

NO BANKING

5 Don't use public computers to make financial transactions. If you do, make sure to log out of the site, and clear the cache and cookies on the computer when you're done.

WHAT IF YOU BECOME A VICTIM?

It's frightening and embarrassing to discover that someone has stolen your identity. But the answer is not to pretend nothing happened and hope that the problem will go away. It won't, and it will only get worse. In fact, the quicker you act, the better your chance of limiting your losses.

The first thing to do is notify one of the three credit agencies and have them place a **fraud alert** on your

report. That way, if someone applies for credit using your name, you'll learn about it before the credit request is granted. Next, tell your bank and credit card company about the problem. Then close any accounts that you didn't open or that show transactions you didn't make.

Also file a police report, and get the report number. You may need this

ON THE TRAIL OF IDENTITY THEFT

When you know the signs of identity theft, you can become your own detective. Start with your statements. If you discover charges that you didn't make, or checks you didn't write, notify the bank or card issuer immediately. Also check your balance whenever you use the ATM. If it's smaller than it should be, find out why. Be sure to keep records of these statements and notifications for future follow-up.

You'll find other clues to identity theft on your credit report. Look for credit card or loan applications that you didn't make. Search for accounts that you don't own. If there is anything you don't recognize, contact the credit agency immediately.

You can get one free report each year from each of the three major credit agencies, Equifax, Experion, or TransUnion at **www.annualcreditreport.com**. It's a good idea to space your requests to the three agencies so you get one every four months. That way, you're getting a free look at your credit report throughout the year.

information later on to help clear up any questions about your credit. Keep copies of all your related correspondence so you can easily prove that you are working hard to get the errors fixed!

And don't forget to file a complaint with the Federal Trade Commission (FTC) to help them track down the thieves www.consumer.ftc.gov/features/feature-0014-identity-theft.

SUSPICIOUS CHARGES

Charges of small amounts on your credit card statement, such as $1 or $5, could be a red flag that an ID thief is testing your card information before they try out a larger purchase. You should also keep a lookout for charges at gas stations, as they can be a signal that your credit information has been compromised.

How to Give Back

You've heard people say that it's better to give than to receive. But what does that really mean?

Many people associate giving with **charity**, and donating money to help those who are in need. But you can also make donations to organizations that support causes that you believe in. There are other kinds of giving as well. For example, you can donate things that you've outgrown or replaced. You can also volunteer your time and special skills and talents.

The point of **philanthropy**, or charitable giving, is not necessarily how much you give. Even small donations can add up to make a big difference. Philanthropy is really about recognizing that others can use your help and then donating what you can to make things better. The good feeling that comes from helping is why many people believe that giving is better, and more rewarding, than receiving.

WHY PEOPLE GIVE

There are many reasons why people give. It may simply be a desire to help others or share their good fortune with them. Or it may be a desire "to give back" to a community, school, or organization that contributed to their success.

Other people believe strongly in a cause, like protecting wildlife, preserving the environment or restoring a community, and they donate time and money to see the cause succeed. Or they may have a very personal reason for giving to an organization that shares their concern, such as stopping unsafe driving or using renewable energy.

YOU CAN HELP!

HOW PEOPLE GIVE

Entertainers hold benefit concerts to raise money for the victims of disasters, such as earthquakes, typhoons, and floods. They are putting the "do" in donate by sharing their time and talent. People attend special dinners and galas to raise money for foundations that research cures for diseases like cancer and diabetes. And some people give a fixed amount of their income, sometimes as much as 10% or more, to the religion of their choice.

Some wealthy people give money to build things that benefit specific communities or society as a whole. For example, they may donate money to build a new hospital wing, community center, or library. Or they may provide scholarships for students going to college.

While you may not have the money at this point in your life to give as much as these major **benefactors**—the people who support major causes and institutions—you can give in more ways that you think.

BUDGETING FOR CHARITY

Just as you budget for things you need and want, you can set aside a portion of your allowance, the money you earn, or gifts you receive, to donate to charity. You can decide how much that should be, depending on your other expenses and how strongly you feel about giving. If you earmark some of your income for charity when creating your budget, you're more likely to have the money available to make your donation.

You might have several different charities that you would like to give to. Here's where budgeting can also help. Think of charity as a short-term, but ongoing goal. By planning how much you would like to donate to each charity, you'll know how much you'll need to save as part of your weekly or monthly budget.

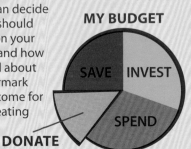

MY BUDGET

SAVE INVEST SPEND DONATE

CHECKING UP ON CHARITIES

There are many worthwhile charities to which you might give time or money. But there are also people who claim to represent charities but really don't. They collect money only to enrich themselves, not to benefit others.

If someone asks you to donate money—in person, by phone, or online—take a closer look before you give. You might go to the organization's website or see what you can find out by typing the charity's name into a search engine. You can also check www.greatnonprofits.com to see a list of recognized charities that you can trust to use your donation for the right purpose.

GIVE AWAY vs. THROW AWAY

Money isn't the only thing you can donate. Some charities specialize in collecting items that you're planning to throw out but are still in useable condition.

For example, there are charities that collect coats and other clothing for those in need. You might donate a jacket that you've outgrown, or shoes that you hardly wore. Other organizations collect used electronic devices, such as phones and computers, which they repair and distribute to people who can't afford them or donate to training programs.

There are neighborhood thrift shops that accept many different items, including books, CDs, and toys. These shops typically give a percentage of the money they earn to charitable organizations, such as food banks, shelters, or other community groups.

VOLUNTEERING: TIME IS MONEY

Besides giving money, you can contribute to charity by **volunteering**, or giving your time. Many charities have small staffs and depend on volunteers to deliver their services and fulfill their mission.

You might volunteer to work in a food or clothing drive to help out the victims of a fire or flood. Or you might volunteer to make a cake for a local bake sale or wash cars to raise money for a school event. During weekends and holidays, you might also volunteer your time in a soup kitchen or at institutions that provide meals for those who would otherwise go hungry.

You can also volunteer to read to younger children or senior citizens in community centers or libraries, or to contribute your time to programs sponsored by your neighborhood church or other religious organization.

While volunteering won't earn you money, it will give you the chance to meet and help other people and to understand the value of philanthropy.

An Awkward Money Moment

GIVING TO A SCAM

A young woman approaches you in the mall, and she seems extremely upset. She explains that her little brother is very sick and she is collecting money to help him get the operation he needs. You give her the last $20 in your wallet, figuring that the little boy needs it more than you do. But then you see the same woman in a different part of the mall, spending your money on a movie ticket. You feel angry, but embarrassed, too.

Helping people is a great thing to do. But when you give money to a person who is being dishonest about where your donation is actually going, you are wasting your money—and not helping those who really need your support. It's best to make sure that a cause or organization is legitimate before you give.

Protection Pays Off

Risks are part of life.

Bikes get stolen, houses flood and people get into fender benders. While the risk of any of these things happening to you is pretty low, the financial consequences are pretty high if something bad does happen to you.

While there is no way to completely eliminate risk, you can help to lessen it. One way is to act responsibly and to take care of yourself and the things you own, especially those that have financial value. Another way is to buy an important financial product called **insurance**, which protects the things that are of value to you.

When you buy insurance, the insurance company will send you a **policy** that describes the things they will pay for in case of accident, illness, or other misfortunes that you could not predict.

HOW INSURANCE WORKS

You pay a fee, or **premium**, to your insurance company for your coverage. If you have an accident or illness, you submit a **claim**, letting the company

know what happened. Depending on the type of coverage you have, and what your policy covers, the insurance company will then pay some or all of your costs.

Even when you have insurance, some costs are your responsibility. Your **deductible** is the amount that you have to pay before the insurance company starts to pay. For example, if there is a fire in your home and you have to make repairs, you may have to cover the first $1,000. After you pay the full amount of the deductible, the insurance company reimburses you for the rest—at least up to the maximum that your policy will pay.

As long as you keep your insurance payments up to date, you are covered. But if you stop paying, your policy **lapses** and your protection is gone.

YOU GET WHAT YOU PAY FOR

In general, the more expensive a policy, the more coverage you have, and the more the insurance company

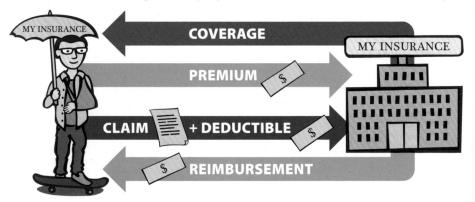

TYPES OF INSURANCE

There are many different kinds of insurance, and each kind is meant to provide a special type of protection:

	AUTO INSURANCE	Covers expenses if you have a car accident and need to repair the car or buy a new one. It also pays the medical costs of someone you accidentally injure when driving a car.
	HOME INSURANCE	Covers some or all of the cost to repair or rebuild your house if it is damaged by fire or other disasters that your policy covers. It also protects any of your possessions that may be stolen.
	RENTERS INSURANCE	Protects your belongings if they are damaged or stolen when you live in an apartment or rented property.
	LIABILITY INSURANCE	Covers some or all of your costs if you are sued because someone is injured on your property, or you injure another person because of something you do.
	HEALTH INSURANCE	Covers some or all of your medical and dental expenses if you get sick or need to stay in the hospital. You may get health insurance from the company you work for or pay for it separately.
	LIFE INSURANCE	Pays a benefit to your family or other people you name in the policy if you die. The money helps replace income you contributed to supporting your family or loved ones while you were living.

will pay for your loss or illness. So when choosing insurance, you should balance how much coverage you need with what you can afford to pay for it.

The insurance company looks at how "risky" you are as an individual to determine what you'll pay for coverage. If you have a safe driving record, for example, you may pay lower rates, which will save you money. But if you've had car accidents or traffic violations, the insurance company may decide that you are a bad risk. As a result, your rates will go up and you'll pay a higher premium, costing you more money. So avoiding risky behavior and activities can be a real money saver.

INSURANCE FOR YOUR MONEY

Remember, you may already have insurance protection for your money. For example, money you have in a bank account is insured by the Federal Deposit Insurance Corporation. And if you have overdraft protection, that's a kind of insurance that if you spend more than you have available in your account, the bank will transfer enough funds to cover any checks you've written or payments you've made.

ACKNOWLEDGMENTS

Special thanks to our editor Mavis Wright and our development partner,
Lightbulb Press, Inc.